The Cornish Saints

Peter Berresford Ellis

Tor Mark Press • Penryn

Other books in the Tor Mark series

China clay — traditional mining methods in Cornwall
Cornish fishing industry — a brief history
Cornish mining industry — a brief history
Cornish folklore
Cornish legends
Cornish mining — underground
Cornish mining — at surface
Cornish recipes
Cornwall's early lifeboats
Cornwall's engine houses
Cornwall's railways
Cornwall's structure and scenery
Customs and superstitions from Cornish folklore
Demons, ghosts and spectres in Cornish folklore
Exploring Cornwall with your car
Harry Carter — Cornish smuggler
Houses, castles and gardens in Cornwall
Introducing Cornwall
Old Cornwall — in pictures
Shipwrecks around Land's End
Shipwrecks around the Lizard
Shipwrecks around Mounts Bay
Shipwrecks — St Ives to Bude
South-east Cornwall
The story of Cornwall
The story of Cornwall's churches
The story of the Cornish language
The story of St Ives
The story of Truro Cathedral
Surfing South-west
Tales of the Cornish fishermen
Tales of the Cornish miners
Tales of the Cornish smugglers
Tales of the Cornish wreckers
Twelve walks on the Lizard
Victorian Cornwall

First published 1992 by Tor Mark Press,
Islington Wharf, Penryn,
Cornwall TR10 8AT

© 1992 Tor Mark Press

ISBN 0-85025-337-3

The cover photograph is by
Andrew Besley of Lelant and is
a detail from the medieval stained glass
at St Neot, showing the saint meeting
the Pope – untypically for a
Cornish saint.

Printed in Great Britain by Swannack Brown & Co Ltd, Hull

Introduction

From the start of the Christian period until Athelstan's conquest in the 10th century, the Christian Church in Cornwall was an integral part of what is now called the 'Celtic Church'. The term is perhaps not strictly accurate, because the early Christian Church among the Celtic peoples was, in most essentials, part of the Roman Catholic Church. Neither can it be said that the 'Celtic Church' was an identifiable organisation with a central leadership in opposition to the Church of Rome.

Nevertheless, for a period of 150 years, during the 5th and 6th centuries, the Celts of the British Isles were cut off from strict Roman influence. While Rome began to reform many of its customs during the 5th century, especially the dating of Easter, the Celts continued to use the old computations and freely mixed many pre-Christian traditions and social concepts into their Christianity, which thus developed as a distinctive culture. Celtic Christianity differed from Rome in its social concepts, philosophies and art forms. Celtic views on land tenure, opposing private ownership and feudal and hereditary rights, their monastic extremism and their asceticism inevitably drew them into conflict with Rome.

It was often claimed by Rome that Celtic Christianity was just an extension of Celtic Druidism, the pre-Christian religion of the Celts. Indeed, in insular Celtic literature, the 'saints' of the Celtic Church are sometimes said to be 'druids' as well as churchmen. It was an accusation levelled at the British Celt Pelagius (AD 354? – 420?) who clashed with Augustine of Hippo over 'predestination'. Pelagius preached that man had Free Will and was responsible for all his acts. Augustine argued that everything was preordained by God and man was not responsible. Pelagius pointed out that this abrogated moral responsibility and opened the way for man to indulge in sin and immorality by claiming that it must have been preordained. Pelagius was accused by Rome of trying to revive Druidic philosophy and declared a heretic. For several hundred years Rome argued that the Celts were riddled with 'Pelagian heresy', demonstrating, I believe, that Pelagius had, indeed, been teaching Celtic moral philosophy.

More accepted by Rome was the Gaulish Celt, Hilary of Poitiers (AD 315? – 367?), the first native Celt to become an outstanding force in the Christian movement. He wrote the first work on the concept of the Holy Trinity, *De Trinitate*. As a Celt, Hilary must have been imbued with the cultural mystic traditions concerning trinity — the triune godship so popular in pre-Christian Celtic worship. As the idea does not occur in Hebrew or Hellenistic thought, it can be argued that the Holy Trinity was a Celtic concept.

During the so-called 'Dark Ages' of Europe, an age of golden enlightenment for the Celtic world, Celtic missionaries took Christian teaching and literacy as far east as the Ukraine, south to southern Italy, north to the Faroes and Iceland and across Europe, founding monasteries, convents and churches. Missionaries of the Celtic Church brought the Faith and literacy to the pagan Anglo-Saxons.

The conflict between Rome and the Celtic Church took many years to resolve; even as late as the 14th century there were still in Scotland bodies of Celtic monks (Culdees — Céle Dé = servants of God) clinging to the traditional forms.

Cornwall, which emerged as a distinct Celtic kingdom after the Saxon conquest of Dumnonia, remained constant to Celtic forms until Athelstan of England began to exert his overlordship and reorganise the church there, creating a diocese of Cornwall with a bishopric at St Germans in the 10th century. Celtic monasticism was on the defensive and the Celtic form of service was abandoned. English overlordship and rule from Canterbury brought in Roman orthodoxy. In AD 1040 the diocese of Cornwall was abolished and not recreated until 1876.

During the 5th–7th centuries, Cornwall was visited by numerous missionaries from Ireland and Wales. It was the custom of the Celtic Church to call all its missionaries and teachers 'Saint', a distinction showing that they were men and women of eminent virtue, holy people preaching Christian doctrines. It did not mean that they had been canonised.

In Cornwall the names of many of these missionaries survive, in place-names and in church dedications. The purpose of this booklet is to list these Celtic saints or missionaries and give some detail of their lives, so far as we know them, and state where their dedications are to be found; this is cross-referenced by a selected gazetteer. The work deals only with Celtic saints and not with the numerous Biblical saints and Early Church fathers such as Blaise, Clement, Dunstan, Faith, Gregory, Lawrence, Michael, Thomas and many others whose dedications are also to be found in Cornwall.

The Celtic Saints of Cornwall

Adwen   This is the Cornish patron saint of sweethearts; a mysterious saint of whom little is known save that she was one of the 24 children of Brychan, King of Powys in the 6th century. Many of the children of Brychan founded churches both in Cornwall and in Devon. Adwen founded her church one mile south of Camelford. Through Anglicisation the place is now called Advent and was mistakenly thought to be named from the Christian calendar. Adwen is also recorded in the form St Athewenna. Her church, which can only be reached by footpath, was rebuilt in 1848 although it still retains a 15th century roof and porch. No feastday has been recorded for Adwen and her rôle in Cornwall, as patron saint of sweethearts, has now been replaced by the more internationally famous male St Valentine.

Allen   Allen, or more popularly Alan, is a Celtic name meaning 'harmony'. An Alan from Wales became bishop of Quimper in Brittany and it is accepted that it was this bishop who gave his name to St Allen, north of Truro. But beyond this, nothing is known of him.

Anta   It is argued that this female saint gave her name to Lelant, presumably after the overthrow of the 5th century Cornish king Tewdrig (Tudor) who had his fortress there. Tewdrig had a nasty habit of welcoming Christian missionaries with martyrdom. Lelant was originally recorded as Lananta — the lan (sacred enclosure or church, equivalent to the Welsh llan) of Anta. A medieval chapel of St Anta still stands. See also St Uny.

Athwenna   See Adwen.

Austell   St Austell (sometimes spelt Austol) and St Mewan had the reputation of being inseparable friends; Mewan became Austell's friend and godfather when he converted to Christianity. Together they studied in a Breton monastery as contemporaries of the famous St Samson (AD490?–565?). Mewan and Austell arrived in Cornwall to preach and the two inseparable friends founded parishes side by side — St Austell and St Mewan. So close were they that when Mewan died, within a week Austell followed him to the grave. Until the Reformation the people of the adjoining parishes named after them preserved the tradition of their friendship by celebrating together. St Austell's feastday was celebrated on 28 June.

Brandwalder   See Breward.

Breaca   This lady was one of three missionaries who arrived from Ireland, Crowan, Germoe and Breaca. At the Hayle Estuary they are said to have escaped the attentions of Tewdrig, the Cornish king who delighted in executing the missionaries, and went on to make their own foundations. In Breaca's case she established a church at Breage, three miles west of Helston.

Breward   A companion of St Samson; his feastday is celebrated on 9 February. He is said to have been a bishop in Jersey, where his feastday is 19 January. Breward gave his name to St Breward, on the east side of Bodmin Moor four miles south of Camelford. His name survives in Brandwalder (thought to be the original form) and in Broladre (in Brittany) and in Brelade (in Jersey).

Brioc   Born in Dyfed in the 6th century, Brioc came on a mission to Cornwall and founded a church at the spot which now bears his name, St Breock, half a mile south-west of Wadebridge. The church today dates in parts from the 13th century. Brioc went on to Brittany where he founded a monastery settlement at a spot which grew into a town and took its name from him as St Brieuc. His feastday is 1 May. Brioc is accredited, in medieval accounts, with numerous friends and disciples. He took no less than 168 followers on one of his missions and 84 on another.

Bryvyth   A tradition at Lanlivery, a hilltop village overlooking the Fowey valley two miles west of Lostwithiel, is that Bryvyth, called Brevita in the Latinised form, was its founding saint. Yet the church here is dedicated to St Manachus of whom nothing is known except that he might have been a friend of Dunstan. See Manacca.

Budoc   According to a surviving medieval Life of this 6th century saint, Budoc was a Breton. His mother Azenor was placed in a great cask at Brest and cast into the sea by her enemies. Adrift in the cask for many months, she gave birth to Budoc and eventually, after five months, they came to the shore of Ireland. Budoc was educated there and sent off on a mission. He visited Dyfed and Cornwall and established a church at Budock, a mile and a half inland from Falmouth pier. Falmouth is a seventeenth century town, and St Budock is its mother church. Budoc set up another establishment at St Budeaux, in Plymouth. He returned to Brittany, according to legend arriving on a floating stone, where, on the retirement of Magloire, he became bishop of Dol. His name in Breton is recorded as Beuzec. His feastday is 8 December.

Buryan   According to the early medieval *Exeter Calendar of Martyrology*, Buryan (who is also recorded as Berriona, Beriana and Beryan) was a young Irishwoman, the daughter of a Munster chieftain, who came to Cornwall in the 5th century and made her foundation at St Buryan, four miles east of Land's End. The English king Athelstan, who first brought Cornwall under English suzerainty, came to her shrine in AD 930 and built a church. Significantly, she is not the only Celtic saint to have her feastday on 1 May, one of the four major pre-Christian Celtic feastdays and usually associated with the female goddess of fertility. The *Calendar of Martyrology* records that Geraint, King of Dumnonia, had a son who was cured of paralysis by prayers to St Buryan. Veryan, south-east of Truro, also takes its name from Buryan, although the church is now dedicated to St Symphorian, one of the martyrs of Gaul who was beheaded at Autun around AD 200.

Cadoc   He lived in the 6th century and is one of the more famous Welsh saints who is widely venerated in South Wales, Cornwall, Brittany and also in Scotland and Ireland. While there is no foundation named after him there is a holy well and chapel at Harlyn Bay near Padstow. Cadoc (also recorded as Cadog) was the founder of Nant Carfan (Llancarfon) where Brendan of Ireland and Malo of Brittany received their training. Written evidence of his life is obscure although he seems to have been a contemporary of Samson and Gildas. Legend has it that he was transported on a cloud to Benevento, Italy, where he was made bishop and met a martyr's death while celebrating Mass.

Carantoc   See Crantock

Cleer   Although St Cleer was not a Celt, being an Englishman named Clarus living in the 8th century, he is worth a mention here for his is a sad and sensational tale. Arriving in Cornwall to preach, he founded his church on the edge of Bodmin Moor, north of Liskeard. The church of St Cleer village is dedicated to him and there is a famous Holy Well with a 5th century cross written in Irish (ogham) characters and another Latin inscribed cross. Less than a mile away is the Doniert Stone which is inscribed: *Doniert rogavit pro anima* (Doniert ordered [this cross] for [the good of] his soul). Doniert is said to be the Cornish king Dungarth who was drowned in AD 875 and who, therefore, may have been a contemporary of Cleer. Cleer was living a saintly life when a local chieftainess fell in love with him. Cleer made it plain that his monastic vows were more important to him than any earthly passions. The lady, upset by the monk's offhand manner, began to pester him. Cleer was forced to head for an isolated hermitage abroad, which became known as St Claire-sur-Epte, but the lady, enraged at being rejected, had him pursued and murdered. His feastday is 4 November.

Clether   Born in the 6th century, Clether is another of the children of Brychan and apart from the fact that he founded a church at St Clether, eight miles west of Launceston, little else is known about him. His feastday survives on 4 November. The chief interest at St Clether is a Holy Well.

Coan   One of the few martyrs of the Celtic Church, a chapel and well dedicated to Coan existed at Merther, where he is patron saint. Merther lies between Tresillian and St Michael Penkevil, on the east side of the Fal River. It is the name which tells the story for *merther* means martyr (although some scholars disagree about this). But why and how Coan met his end we do not know.

Colan   Colan's feastday was celebrated on 20 May. While a medieval life of Colan in Welsh has survived, the stories are in the realms of fantasy and the same tales are ascribed to other saints. A Welshman, his name is found in Llangollen, Clwyd, and in Langolen in Brittany. In Cornwall, the saint left his name in Colan, three miles east of Newquay, where the church is dedicated to him.

Columb   The Irish name Colm, meaning 'a dove', has given us a common Christian name in its Latinised form Columba, used by both male and female. Colmcille (521? – 597), 'Colm of the Cell', the Donegal saint who preached in Ireland and Scotland, was the first Colm (Columba) from whom other saints, such as the Spanish female Columba of Córdova (died AD 853), took their names. In Cornwall, the tradition of the St Columba who is the patron saint of both St Columb Major and St Columb Minor, is extraordinarily close to the tradition of Columba of Córdova. The story is that Columba was a Christian girl who rejected the advances of a pagan suitor. She refused his demand to renounce her faith and he beheaded her. The act is said to have taken place at Ruthvos in St Columb Major. The place name might seem to confirm the act for *ruth* is red and *vos* is a form of *fos* — a wall. The 'red wall' signifying the spot where the beheading took place. This type of story is fairly common and associated with other Christian maidens in other places. Similar beheadings of St Columba of Córdova and St Columba of Sens indicate that the story has no value in history.

Conan   The patron of the church at Washaway, an Anglicisation of Egloshayle — church by the estuary — may have been a Conan known to have associated with St Petroc. A rival claim is that the church takes its patronage from a Cornishman chosen by Athelstan to be the first bishop of his foundation at St Germans in AD 931. A feastday is celebrated on 23 July.

Congar   This saint has survived as the patron of a small chapel at Lanivet, two miles south-west of Bodmin, and also as the farm name St Ingonger. A contemporary of Cadoc and Petroc, he is more venerated in Somerset where an imaginative Life was written at Wells in the early Middle Ages.

Constantine   A Scottish account says that Constantine was a Cornish king, bearing a Roman name. This was not uncommon, for Scotland had several kings named Constantine, Constantine I (863 – 877), Constantine MacBeth (900 – 942) and Constantine III (995 – 997). Constantine abdicated in favour of his son after the death of his wife and went to Ireland, where he became a monk. He had been converted by St Petroc. He was working at a monastic mill when his identity was discovered; he volunteered to join Colmcille's work in Scotland and is said to have become Scotland's first martyr, becoming venerated in Scotland, Wales and Cornwall. He gave his name to the parish of Constantine, five miles south-west of Falmouth, at the head of a creek by the Helford river estuary, and to Constantine Bay.

Corentin   The name survives in Cury, on the Lizard four miles south of Helston. St Corentin's church is Norman, although a more ancient cross survives there. Corentin is one of the more famous Breton saints. He was the first bishop of Quimper, which was known as Quimper-Corentin until the French Revolution began its attack on the Church. His feastday is 12 December.

Crantock   According to a Life written in Wales, King Arthur asked Crantock, sometimes called Carantoc, to rid the land of a marauding dragon. The saint captured the beast and prevented Arthur's warriors from killing it; it was released on condition that it behaved itself in future. Crantock seems to have been the son of Ceredig, who gave his name to Ceredigion (Cardigan). He was an assistant of St Patrick in Ireland and is venerated in Somerset as well as at Carantec in Brittany and Crantock, on the south side of the Gannel estuary near Newquay. His Holy Well is still to be seen, although the church is Norman.

Crida   Little is known of Crida except that she was a woman; her name survives in the form of Creed, a church south of Grampound, six miles west of St Austell. Sancreed in West Penwith is not associated with her, Sancreed being a full name. Crida may be associated with Crediton, Devon, and may also appear as St Grada on the Lizard.

Crowan   The companion of Breaca and Germoe; her name survives at Crowan, a village south of Camborne. Archaeologists have traced a round chapel and dwelling there, which may be the original.

Cubert   Cubert gave his name to a village south-west of Newquay, looking out over the dunes of Penhale to the sea. The church is dedicated to him and in its grounds is a 7th century stone carved with the words *Conetoci fili tegerno mali,* commemorating the death of Tegerno's son Conetocius. St Cubert's Holy Well is in a cave, reached only at low tide, at the north end of Holywell Bay. In the 14th century there was confusion with St Cuthbert of Lindisfarne (634? – 687) but Cubert was actually Gwbert of Ceredigion in Dyfed.

Cuby   Cuby is said to have been the son of St Selevan and is rare among Cornish saints as being Cornish born of a Cornish family. His church stands on the parish boundary between Cuby and Tregony. The church has a 6th or 7th century inscribed stone *Nonnita Ercilini Rigati . . . Tris Fili Ercilini,* 'Nonnita, Ercilinus, Rigatus, the three sons of Ercilinus'. Cuby went to Ireland and then to Wales where he was acclaimed as 'one of the makers of Christian Wales'. His great foundation was at Holyhead on Holy Island, off Ynys Mon (Anglesey). Here he was known as Kebi. His name also survives in Caergybi. His feastday is celebrated on 12 December.

Dei   It may be that St Day is the same as St Dei of western Brittany. In Cornwall a parish dedicated to him stands east of Redruth, formed out of part of Gwennap.

Dewi   Dewi Sant or St David is honoured at Davidstow, north of Bodmin Moor. He is the patron saint of Wales and lived in the 6th century. There is no record that Dewi Sant actually visited Cornwall but, interestingly, not far from the dedication at Davidstow is a dedication to his mother Non at Altarnun (Non's Altar) which may suggest a connection with the saint's family. His feastday is 1 March.

Docco   Docco came to Cornwall from Gwent in south Wales with his sister, Kew; jointly they founded a religious centre at St Kew which was originally called Lan Docco. It was to Lan Docco that St Samson, with his family and followers, first went on landing in Cornwall. The *Life of St Samson* says that Samson was greeted with humility and hospitality by the religious; their spokesman was Junavius, whose name meant 'Light' in the Cornish language. This seems to imply that Docco and Kew were dead or no longer in charge by this time, early in the 6th century.

Elwyn   In spite of his Brythonic Celtic name, he is said to have come over from Ireland and in some sources is claimed as a companion of Breaca. He landed in Porthleven, which name derives from 'Porth-Elwyn', the landing place or harbour of Elwyn. A chapel was dedicated to him there. When Hayle expanded, and a new church was built (its parish church remains Phillack) it was dedicated to him.

Endelienta   Patron saint of St Endellion, four miles north of Wadebridge, she was another of the children of Brychan of Wales who came to Cornwall in the 6th century to preach. According to Nicholas Roscarrock (who lived at St Endellion in Tudor times) the saint's tomb was defaced during the reign of Henry VIII. Thanks to Roscarrock, however, the altar-tomb has been identified and preserved. Her feastday is 29 April and there were two wells in the parish which bore her name. A mile away was a 6th or 7th century carved stone *XP Brocagni hic iacit nadotti filius* — Brocagnus the son of Nadottus lies here.

Enoder   Nothing is known of this saint who gave his name to St Enoder, six miles east of Newquay.

Enodoc   Not to be confused with Enoder, Enodoc seems to have been someone of prominence in connection with Bodmin Priory. A church dedicated to him stands on the right bank of the Camel Estuary, near Padstow. The church is basically Norman, and was for many years buried in the dunes.

Erbyn   Also recorded as Ervan, he is said to have been the father of St Selevan. His name is remembered in the village of St Ervan, where the church was originally dedicated to him. However, in recent years the dedication has become confused with St Erme, the Greek saint and martyr Hermes.

Erc   See Erth.

Erney   Also known as Terney; nothing is known of this saint to whom a parish near St Germans, and another at North Hill, just east of Bodmin near the Lynher River, are dedicated. The latter church bears the name Torney, but this seems to have been an incorrect transcription of the Latin recording of the name — Terninus. It has been suggested that Erney or Terney could be the same person as St Ternan, the 5th century missionary to the Pictish kingdom. However, the name was popular at this period; Tigernonos means 'king'. Most famously it occurs in the Mabinogion as Teyrnon, foster father to Pryderi.

Erth   St Erc, to give the proper form, was converted by St Patrick who made him Bishop of Slane. He was one of a group of Irish missionaries who came to the Hayle estuary and who is now commemorated there in the village which bears his name. He is said to have been the brother of St Ia and St Euny.

Euny   Usually given as Uny, brother of St Erc (Erth) and St Ia; one of the Irish missionaries led by Gwinear who landed at Hayle. He is patron of Redruth as well as Lelant and is associated with Crown and Sancreed. Significantly, his feastday fell on 1 February, one of the four major pagan Celtic festivals, usually associated with the goddess of fertility. The indications are that he was martyred, for in Wendron parish there existed an ancient and important church dedicated as Merther Uny (Martyred Uny). However, some scholars believe that merther indicates a place where relics were kept, not a martyrdom.

Eval   Nothing is known of the saint whose name is now best remembered in the name of an RAF aerodrome which played a notable part during World War II. The church dedicated to him still serves the air station. One tradition is that Eval was a Breton missionary in Cornwall, listed in 1290 as Uvel.

Ewe   Recorded as a female saint, although some believe her to be the Breton male saint, St Eo. She is remembered at the parish which bears her name, St Ewe.

Feock   Feock presents us with rather a problem as some early medieval calendars give the name in feminine form - Sancta Feoca, while at the village of Feock, on a peninsula between Restronguet Creek and the upper part of Carrick Roads, the saint is thought to be masculine. It is recorded that the image of Feock in a stained glass window which used to exist there was that of a male. Some have said that he was one and the same person as St Maeoc, a hermit of Brittany.

Fili   Fili was honoured in Wales, where he probably originated. He gave his name to Philleigh, not far from King Harry Ferry on the bank of the Fal. He was said to be a companion of St Kea (q.v.). Kea stands opposite Philleigh on the other bank of the Fal; in Devon, just east of Barnstaple, the two saints' names appear again in Landkey (Lan of Kea) and Filleigh. Their names are associated again in Brittany.

Fimbarrus   A Cornish rendition of the famous Irish saint Finbarr, abbot-bishop of Cork (died c. 633) He was said to be a native of Connacht but conducted his missionary work in Munster, founding the monastery and episcopal see of Cork. He is associated with Dewi Sant, with whom he was supposed to have made a pilgrimage to Rome. One account claims that he crossed the Irish Sea on horseback. Tradition has it that the saint arrived at Fowey, where the church is named after him. The church was later, through habit, called St Barry's and in 1336 Bishop Grandisson of Exeter, in the belief it was founded by St Nicholas of Bari, rededicated it. But the name has reverted to St Fimbarrus. A confusion arose through a claim that Barry was one of the children of Brychan and an uncle of St Cadoc. However, a shortening of the name Finbarr is not uncommon: Barra in the Outer Hebrides, where Finbarr founded Cille Bharra, was named from him. His feastday is September 25. While the Irish claim he is buried at Cloyne, the Cornish claim he is buried at Fowey.

Gennys   There is a St Gennys in north-east Cornwall and he may well have been a local saint. But the parish now accepts that it is dedicated to a Celtic saint of Gaul, Genesius (Genès) of Arles, in Provence. He was martyred about AD 250 when, as a clerk in the Roman administration, he refused to write out a Government edict against Christians on the grounds he was one himself. He was pursued and arrested and beheaded on the banks of the Rhône. His cult became widespread, with a feastday on 25 August. However, 2 May is celebrated in Cornwall, prompting the idea that there may have been another saint named Gennys.

Gerent   The name is clearly the same as Geraint, which was, indeed still is, a popular name. 'St Gerent' has become the patron of Gerrans, on the east side of Roseland, just inland from Porthscatho. Tradition is utterly confusing: we are told that there was a king of Cornwall whose fortress was at Dingerein, where a mound lies beside the main road one and a half miles north of the village. Was he one and the same as Geraint, king of Dumnonia (of which Cornwall was then the western half) to whom St Adhelm wrote a letter in AD 704, attacking the Celtic king for his adherence to Celtic Christianity? There was another Geraint of Dumnonia who rode with the Gododdin in their famous attack on the English at Caertraeth (Catterick), where Arthur has his first mention in literature and thus, in later tales, a Sir Geraint emerges as one of Arthur's Knights of the Round Table. Do all the tales of Geraint, popular in Wales and in Brittany, belong to the same man, or were they different men? For there is a 'Gerent' who emerges as one of five generations of 'saints': Lud, whose son was St Gerent, whose son was St Erbyn, whose sons were St Just and St Selevan, whose son was St Cuby.

Germanus   St Germans was the site of the ancient cathedral of Cornwall and remained so until 1043 when, following the English reorganisation of the Cornish Church the see was transferred to Crediton in Devon and shortly afterwards to Exeter. Church and village took their name from the Gaulish bishop Germanus of Auxerre (378? – 448). Germanus was elected bishop of Auxerre in 418 and was twice sent to Britain where the Roman church was disturbed by what they called Pelagian heresy (see page 3). St Germanus is said to have taught St Patrick and St Illtud, and to have visited Cornwall where he made the foundation named after him. His feastday is 31 July.

Germoe   Germoe is recorded as an Irish missionary who landed at Hayle with Breaca and Crowan. The village of Germoe, halfway between Helston and Marazion, takes its name from him. There is a 15th century building in the churchyard called St Germoe's Chair, which is a triple seat of stone, with arches above like sedilia, under a little gable and two pointed arches. In medieval times, Germoe was also referred to as a 'king'. Did the Irishman arrive in Cornwall and find himself ruler of the local people or was it a courtesy title?

Gluvias   Gluvias is the patron of St Gluvias by Penryn. A Welshman, he is said to have been the brother of Cadoc and a nephew of Petroc. His feastday is 3 May.

Gonand   The patron of the church of Roche, St Gonand, is a mysterious character and there are no surviving records of him. It is thought, therefore, that the name may be a misrepresentation of Conan. The village of Roche, five miles north of St Austell, contains a Holy Well, situated a mile north of the village, and in the churchyard there is an old cross. The village takes its name from a spectacular freak of nature to the south, Roche Rocks (*roche* meaning rock in French), a group of huge, rugged fangs up to 100 ft in height. On top of the largest, reached only by iron ladders, is a two-chambered chapel built in 1409 and dedicated to St Michael. It is believed to have been a dwelling of monastic hermits.

Goran   According to the medieval *Life of St Petroc*, St Wron was the original form of Goran. He was a hermit at Bodmin who gave Petroc shelter and hospitality when he visited there. He then left Petroc in charge and went off to seek a new place to dwell, leaving his name at St Guron's Well in Bodmin churchyard. He apparently settled at Goran, two miles south of Mevagissey, which has Goran Haven and Goran Churchtown.

Gueryr   A saint whose shrine was at St Neot, on the southern edge of Bodmin Moor. It was visited by Alfred the Great of England (871 – 902), according to the Welsh monk, Asser. Asser was adviser to the English king and is credited with codifying English Law. Apart from the reference to Gueryr and the fact that the remains of St Neot were also buried with him, nothing is known of this saint.

Gulval   Latin usage mutates Gw and Gu to W and so we have the name Wolvela as the patron saint of Gulval, half a mile from the sea north-east of Penzance. In this form the name is feminine and in the parish there is Bosulval, 'Dwelling Place of Wolvela', which might signify her original foundation. In the 15th century churchyard there are traces of an early occupation with a 6th or 7th century stone engraved '*Quenatauci ic Dinui Filius*'.

Gunwalloe   The 6th century patron of Gunwalloe on the west coast of the Lizard, Winwaloe, would have had a G as initial letter in Celtic; the place name Gunwalloe is therefore nearer the original name than the church dedication. In Brittany the name survives as Guénolé. He was a friend of Budoc and according to a 9th century Life written at Landévennec he came of a Cornish family which had settled in Brittany, where Gunwalloe was born. He played an important role in Breton religious life, founding the great monastery at Landévennec, in Cornouaille, Brittany. He then came to Cornwall where he is credited with the foundation of a monastery at Landewednack. That name is thought to have derived from the lan or church enclosure of Gunwalloe, although some argue that it was named after a St Winoc; but there is no evidence for the existence of a saint of that name. Landewednack certainly seems to be derived from the Breton Landévennec. It is thought that Gunwalloe was also patron of Towednack, West Penwith, and Tremaine, near Egloskerry, four miles west of Launceston. His feastday is 3 March.

Gwennap While the name Gwennap survives in the village three miles south-east of Redruth, originally Lanwennap, the saint's name has come to be written as Wennap due to the medieval Latin loss of the initial G. The name is feminine but nothing is known about her.

Gwinear A 6th century Irish martyr whose feastday is 23 March. *A Life of St Gwinear* written about the 14th century records that he led a group of Irish missionaries to Cornwall. They landed at the mouth of the Hayle where the ruler, Tewdrig (Tudor), put Gwinear and some of his companions to death. Others escaped. Tewdrig appears in the *Life of Meryadoc* as a Muslim, which obviously was not the case. Henry Jenner suggested that he was probably a Christian who simply resented incursions by 'foreign' missionaries. It has been suggested by other sources that Gwinear was not Irish at all but a Welshman who came to Cornwall with Meriadoc and afterwards went to Brittany, where he is venerated as St Guigner at Pluvigner where his legend is adopted to local conditions.

Gwithian Gwithian or Gothian was patron of the hamlet which bears his name, some three miles north-east of Hayle. Nothing is known of the saint. Somewhere along the wild extent of shoreline in the region near the Red River, buried in shifting dunes, is an oratory said to be an ancient Celtic one, some 50ft long and 20ft wide. It was revealed and excavated in the 19th century but has been allowed to disappear again.

Hydroc A Bodmin Calendar, dated 1478, includes an entry for St Ydrocus, whose feastday fell on 5 May. He gave his name to Lanhydrock, between Bodmin and Lostwithiel. The church is dedicated to him. In the churchyard is an ancient Celtic cross standing eight feet high with interlacings carved on it. It is reported to have once had a wheeled head.

Ia More popularly known as St Ive, she was an Irishwoman, the daughter of a Munster chieftain, and is said to have travelled to Cornwall with the group led by Gwinear. She escaped the executions by Tewdrig and found a patron in a local chieftain named Dinan. Could this be the same man mentioned in the inscription at Gulval? In another medieval tale, Ia came to Cornwall by herself, seated on a giant leaf. This may not be totally far fetched; anyone who has seen the traditional Irish boat, the currach, will know how much it resembles a leaf on the water. Dinan built a church for Ia at the spot which bears her name, St Ives in west Cornwall, which is called in Cornish Porth Ia. Her feastday is 3 February. The St Ives in Cambridgeshire is named not after St Ia, but after St Ivo, as is St Ive in east Cornwall.

Ildierna   According to William of Worcester, who visited Cornwall in the 15th century, the remains of a bishop named St Hyldren were enshrined in the church of Lansallas, two and a half miles west of Polperro. Significantly, his feastday was on 1 February, one of the great Celtic festivals. Nothing is known about Ildierna or Hyldren, not even the sex for the Latin name has a feminine ending implying that Ildierna was a woman.

Illogan   William of Worcester recorded that the remains of St Illogan were still preserved and honoured in the 15th century. Nothing is known of the saint who gave his name to Illogan two miles north-west of Redruth. The old church here was demolished in 1849 and the new one is built a distance away from the original site.

Issy   Issy or Issey is listed as one of the children of Brychan and gives his name to St Issey on the main road between Wadebridge and Padstow. He is also half of Mevagissey which derives from *'Meva hag Issey'*, *hag* being Cornish for 'and'. The church is dedicated to Saints Meva (see St Mevan) and Issey. It is believed that there has been a church on the same site since about AD 500.

Ivo   Not to be confused with Ia, Bishop Ivo had, according to legend, his origins in east Cornwall and gives his name to Saint Ive (pronounced Eve) between Liskeard and Callington and also St Ives in Cambridgeshire (formerly Huntingdonshire). About AD 1000 some bones and a bishop's insignia were found at the village of Slepe which was renamed St Ives and became (with the benefit of the saintly connection) a thriving medieval town. The bones were taken to Ramsey Abbey. His feastday is April 24. The Cambridgeshire tradition is that he was a Persian bishop, who took up residence at Slepe and died there c. 600.

Juliot   Juliot, whose name appears in varying guises as Julitta, Gilt and Juliana, is listed as one of the children of Brychan. Her name is remembered at Lanteglos, by Camelford, and at St Juliot near Boscastle. She is also claimed as the patron of the chapel on the 'Island' (headland) at Tintagel by the medieval castle. It is thought she was connected with the monastery there. Her feastday is 16 June.

Just   The church of St Just-in-Penwith is a 15th century building. When William of Worcester visited it he noted that it was claimed that the church enshrined the relics of St Just. The church is certainly far older than the 15th century and retains a stone bearing the Chi-Ro symbol (XP) and the words *'Selus Ic Iacit'*. This is dated to the 5th or 6th century. Just, given as Justin or Yestin, was a son of St Geraint. He gives his name not only to St Just-in-Penwith (which has a famous *Plen-an-gwarry* [place of the plays], where the Cornish medieval miracle plays were performed) but to St-Just-in-Roseland, on the east side of Carrick Roads, where the church is placed in one of the most attractive settings in Cornwall.

Kea   The inseparable friend of Fili; he gave his name to Kea opposite Philleigh on the Fal. He is reported to have been a friend of Gildas (c.500 – c.570) who is famous as the author of *De excidio et conquestu Britanniae* (Concerning the Ruin and Conquest of Britain). Gildas is said to have been from the Strathclyde British (Celtic) kingdom and to have travelled extensively in the Celtic lands, ending his life in Brittany where he is credited with founding the monastery at Rhuys. Kea is said to have visited the monastery at Cleder in Brittany and on his return was instrumental in trying to make a peace between Arthur and Mordred. Kea, it seems, appears in Arthurian legend in the guise of Sir Kay, Arthur's steward. His feastday is 3 October.

Kenwyn   Whether there was a St Kenwyn, who gave his name to the picturesque church near Truro, or whether Kenwyn is merely a misrecording of St Keyne (with the Cornish wyn/gwyn — white/pure added to her name) is impossible to say.

Keria   The patron of Egloskerry — the church of Keria — four miles west of Launceston, was one of the daughters of Brychan but little else is known about her.

Keverne   On the east coast of the Lizard peninsula stands the village bearing the saint's name. There was a Celtic monastery there in the Middle Ages. Of the saint little is known except a legend in which St Just is accused of stealing Keverne's paten, or communion plate. Just only gives up the plate when Keverne pursues him with great boulders, which can still be seen lying where they fell on Tremenheverne Downs. In this place name 'Keverne' mutates — changes its grammatical form — to 'heverne'. Thus the name means 'the place of the stones of Keverne'. The story is told in the rhyme of 'The Good St Keverne and the Gaunt St Just'. The village of St Keverne, incidentally, is best known as the place from which the blacksmith Myghal Josef 'An Gof' (The Smith) led the great Cornish uprising against Henry VII, in 1497. An Gof and the Cornish army were defeated on Blackheath near London having marched successfully to within a mile or two of the city.

Kew   Three miles north-east of Wadebridge stands the village which takes its name from this saint. It was originally called Lan Docco, for the monastery of Docco (q.v.) was said to have stood here. Kew was the sister of Docco and shared his mission. Until the 15th century a chapel dedicated to St Kew stood outside the church but was given up as part of an enlargement of the church when the entire place took her name. Her feastday is 8 February.

Keyne   This daughter of Brychan (6th century) was possessed of a wicked sense of humour because she endowed a Holy Well, a half mile south-east of St Keyne's village, with the power of granting dominance in a marriage partnership. Tradition has it that she was a beautiful but eccentric virgin. The name is cognate with the word *cain* (beautiful). Along with her brothers and sisters she took herself off south of the Severn to evangelise. Some enthusiasts have seen her name in the name Keynsham, near Bristol, although this name actually derives from Caegin's hamm, or homestead. Keyne eventually set up home at St Keyne between Looe and Liskeard and at the crossroad by the well she is said to have waylaid travellers and converted them, although a 14th century tradition maintains she was a recluse. Her feastday is 8 October. The English romantic poet and Poet Laureate Robert Southey (1774–1843) celebrated St Keyne with a very mediocre piece about a married couple seeking the gift of St Keyne's well:

> I hastened as soon as the wedding was o'er
> And left my good wife in the porch,
> But i' faith she had been wiser than me
> For she took a bottle to church.

Ladoca   A saint remembered only in the name of a holy well at a farm at Ladock.

Levan   See Selevan.

Ludgvan   The village of Ludgvan (pronounced Lu'djan) stands two miles north-west of Marazion. There is some argument as to whether the name is a simple place-name or whether it comes from a saint. The latter argument has strong evidence as some documents record the place as St Ludgvan and forms of the name such as Lewdegran and Ludewon are also recorded. Today the Ludgvan Feast celebrates St Lewdegran. The church was rebuilt in the 15th century when the dedication was changed to St Paul, celebrating his conversion on 25 January. But a very ancient carving of a patronal figure built into the porch would indicate an earlier veneration.

Mabyn   Mabyn was one of the daughters of Brychan. She is the patron of St Mabyn near Wadebridge. According to Nicholas Roscarrock, at the time the church was built in the early 16th century a hymn to Mabyn was popular. She appears in the windows of St Neot's church nearby. Perhaps a little irreverently she appears on the sign of St Mabyn Inn, the local Free House. Her feastday is 18 November.

Madron   The church at Madron, named after the saint, has its dedication to Madron in the guise of St Madernus. Madron also survives in Madron's Well, now regarded as a wishing well, and St Madron's Baptistery nearby. But the real identity of the saint is a mystery. It has been claimed he was either the Welsh Saint Padarn or the Irish Saint Madran, the latter being a claimant for the foundation of Tréguier abbey and monastery in Brittany. His feastday is 17 May.

Manacca   A 10th century Celtic saint who worked with St Dunstan (c.909 – 988), Archbishop of Canterbury. Dunstan, born in Glastonbury, was related to the royal family of Wessex and was a principal advisor to the Wessex kings. Dunstan and Manacca are the joint patrons of Lanreath. Little is known of Manacca although he is pictured in a medieval window at St Neot and is mentioned as founding Manaccan, near Helford.

Mawes   Apart from the fact that Mawes was associated with St Budoc and is venerated more in Brittany, at le Maudez and Lanmodez, little is known of the saint who gave his name to St Mawes village, opposite Falmouth on the west side of the Roseland peninsula. Various traditions have him either as a Welshman or an Irishman who settled here by a holy well, which still exists near the Victory Inn, to live a life of contemplation watching the setting sun. His feastday was on 18 November.

Mawgan   A 6th century Welsh missionary who was associated with Cadoc and Brioc. His name is also known in Brittany and appears variously as Maugan and Meugan. His name is given to the beautiful Vale of Mawgan or Lanherne, north-east of Newquay where Mawgan-in-Pydar stands; the current church has a 13th century tower but is said to have been built over an old Celtic monastery. Catholicism never died out in this vale and today there is a Carmelite foundation here. St Mawgan also gives his name to Mawgan-in-Meneage, four miles south-east of Helston. Some versions of his life say he was a pupil of St Patrick of Ireland but that would have precluded his being contemporary with Cadoc and Brioc. His feastday is 24 September.

Mawnan   St Mawnan is joint patron of the church at Mawnan with St Stephen, the first martyr of the Christian Church at Jerusalem (died c.AD 35). Stephen was venerated is several parts of Cornwall, for example at Launceston (Lanstefan) and Saltash. Mawnan was obviously a local Celtic saint but how his name was coupled with the Biblical saint is not known.

Mellion   The patron of St Mellion in east Cornwall was a Breton, St Melaine, who was chosen to succeed St Amand, Bishop of Rennes, in the late 5th century. He was an influential person with a reputation for wisdom and piety, and was respected by Clovis (481 – 511), the rapacious king of the Franks who became converted to Christianity. Melaine was buried at Rennes and his feastday is 6 November. He was honoured in Cornwall not only at St Mellion but at Mullion (q.v.) where the original saint, with a similar name, became forgotten as the cult of Melaine took over. St Mellons in south Wales also takes its name from him.

Merryn   The Celtic patron of St Merryn, two and a half miles from Padstow, was almost lost for in the Middle Ages the name become identified with Marina, whose father became a monk in Bithynia and kept her with him, disguising her as a boy. On his death she continued to live undetected in the monastery although her sex was discovered on her death. Marina's feastday is 12 February. However the Cornish feastday is 7 July, reinforcing the impression that a Celtic saint named Merryn was venerated prior to the confusion with Marina. Indeed, Merryn can be identified with the Welsh and Breton saint Merin who is remembered in the place-names Llanferin and Bodferin.

Merteriana   Patron of the lonely Forrabury church situated on the cliff top at Trevena near Tintagel, Merteriana was venerated at Minster church, the mother church of nearby Boscastle, which once held her shrine. While William de Botreaux is generally regarded as founding the monastery from which the Minster church grew, some say that the church at Trevena was the original chapel for the monastic settlement. Her feastday is 9 April.

Meryadoc   A 6th century bishop and patron saint of Camborne whose name is also recorded as Meriadec and Meriasek. The church at Camborne takes its dedication from him and even in recent times people from the parish were known as 'merry geeks' and 'merry jacks'. Meryadoc is one of the best known of Cornish Celtic saints: there are several traditions about him. One says he was a companion of Gwinear and therefore an Irish missionary, among those who landed at Hayle and met Tewdrig. Certainly it is interesting that the names of Meryadoc and Gwinear are found next to each other at Camborne and Gwinear and, indeed, the names are also found close together at Pontivy, Brittany. Meryadoc is also venerated in Brittany as the bishop of Vannes. The saint is now best known as the subject of the play *Bewnans Meryasek* (Life of St Meryasek) which is the only full-length medieval saint's play to survive in the Cornish language. In the play, Meryadoc comes from Brittany and confronts Tewdrig in a series of arguments on Christianity. Warned of the perfidy of the man, he escapes to Brittany, hiding from his pursuers under Carrek Veryasek (Meryasek's

Rock) which, while not known today, was clearly known to audiences of the play in the 16th century. The play, indeed, is full of local allusions and replete with symbolic wonders. It is thought to have been written in 1504 by Father Rad(olphus) Ton, the parish priest of Crowan near Camborne.

Meubred   Reported to be a hermit from Ireland, Meubred is the patron of the church at Cardingham, on the edge of Bodmin Moor. There are a number of inscribed stones in the churchyard dating to the 6th and 7th centuries and a carved cross from the 9th century, nearly 9ft high, and inscribed. Nothing else is known of Meubred except that he was honoured in medieval times and can be seen depicted in one of the stained glass windows of St Neot's church where he appears with St Mabyn.

Mevan   Sometimes called Meva, this saint is thought to be the same person as Mewan. If he was an different person, then all that is known is that he shares a joint dedication at Mevagissey (Meva-hag-Issey).

Mewan   A 6th century saint thought to be the same person as Mevan (above). He is reported, in a *Life of St Mewan,* to have been a friend and godfather of Austell (q.v.). He also appears in the guise of St Méen in Brittany. He and Austell studied with Samson there and evangelised the Brocéline district, which figures in Arthurian romances, and founded Paimpont, a famous monastery. A church still survives at the village of St Mewan but it mainly dates from the 16th century. Here his relics are still enshrined. He is also honoured in Normandy and elsewhere in France because it was thought that waters, dedicated in his name, healed skin diseases. He is also said to have caused a fountain to gush miraculously at the monastery of Gael, in Brittany. Mewan is said to have come from Gwent, in south Wales, and was a relative of Samson, whom he accompanied to Cornwall and Brittany. He foretold his own death and when he died, it was reported that his body remained uncorrupted, enshrined in an aura of fragrance, until St Austell died and joined him. St Mewan is now almost absorbed by the growth of the town of St Austell where once they were entirely separate parishes. Mewan's feastday is 21 June.

Minver   Yet another of the children of Brychan, her name occurs as Menefreda and other forms. The name survives in the village three miles north of Wadebridge where the present church dates from the 13th century only. According to Nicholas Roscarrock, who in the 16th century saw her hermitage, chapel and holy well at Tredrizzick, one popular tale was that an assault was made on Minver by Satan when she was combing her hair. She threw her comb at the Devil and he fled. Her feastday is on 24 November.

Morenna   The saint who gave his name to Lamorran is said to be identical with the Breton saint Moren mentioned in Gospatrick's Charter of c.1060.

Morwenna   Morwenstow is the northernmost parish in Cornwall. There is no village but only a church dedicated to St Morwenna which is of ancient foundation. A document of 1246 refers to it as an old building. The present church dates from Norman times and is a fascinating structure. The place was made famous in the 19th century by its mildly eccentric vicar/poet the Rev. R.S. Hawker.

Mullion   This could be the Breton saint known as St Mollien, although there is some confusion and later accounts identify him with a St Melaine or St Melan who came to be the patron of St Mellion in east Cornwall (q.v.). Mollien was the original patron of Mullion on the west coast of the Lizard peninsula.

Mylor   The patron of Mylor, a church and village two miles north of Falmouth, and also of Linkinhorne, this saint is said to have been a Breton abbot-bishop, remembered in Brittany as St Meloir. There is also a dedication at Amesbury in Wiltshire to a Saint Melor who seems to be one and the same person.

Nectan   One of Brychan's more famous children, credited with being the eldest son. His name is found in Cornwall, Brittany and also in Devon. In Cornwall there is St Nectan's Glen near Tintagel, and St Nectan's Kieve, a waterfall under which the saint is said to have been buried. St Nectan's chapel near Lostwithiel is under the care of St Winnow parish. Also St Nighton (recorded as St Nictan in 1284) takes it name from the saint. According to a Life of Nectan, the saint lived at Hartland Abbey, Devon, where his brothers and sisters, who had settled in Cornwall, would come to visit him and discuss the work of their mission. His feastday was 17 June. According to his Life, two robbers attempted to steal Nectan's cows and when the saint attempted to stop them and, incidentally, convert them to Christianity, they beheaded him and he thus became a martyr.

Neot   Neot was a 9th century Cornish saint who studied at Glastonbury and then became a hermit in Cornwall. His name survives in St Neot, although the original saint venerated here was Gueryr (q.v.). The name is also said to be part of Menheniot: 'sanctuary of Neot' has been suggested. A *Life of St Neot*, no longer extant, is the origin of the story of Alfred burning the cakes. According to Asser, the Welsh monk and advisor to Alfred, Neot was associated with the English king. Neot's feastday is 31 July.

According to tradition, Neot's remains were stolen to grace a new priory at Eynesbury near Huntingdon (and coincidentally near St Ives!), where the monks then founded a new town called St Neots. King Edgar and the powerful Bishop of Ely colluded in this theft; a band of Cornishmen tracked the relics to Eynesbury and tried to bring them back, but were repelled by the King's men.

Neulina   Neulina is remembered in the name Newlyn East, near Newquay and Perranporth, but not in Newlyn near Penzance, where the name is differently derived. The church at Newlyn East is dedicated to her and local tradition says she was martyred here. But a Breton tale speaks of a lady called Noluen who, with her companion, crossed from Cornwall on a leaf and was martyred near Pontivy.

Nevet   The patron of Lanivet, a small village two miles south- west of Bodmin, is probably one and the same as Nevet founder of Lannevet in Brittany. In the south porch of the church is a pillar stone dating from the 6th century, carved with the name 'Annicu'. Several other carved stones date from the period up to the 10th century.

Non   Non or Nonna was the mother of the famous Dewi Sant, the patron saint of Wales. Her name survives in Altarnun, seven miles south-west of Launceston, on the edge of Bodmin Moor. The church is dedicated to St Nonna and stands not far from Davidstow which is dedicated to her son, Dewi. Her feastday is 15 June.

Pattern   There are two traditions for the man who gave his name to North and South Petherwin, one on each side of Launceston. Firstly, that he was a local chieftain whose son became St Constantine (q.v.) or secondly that he was the Welsh abbot-bishop St Padarn who went on to Brittany and established the monastery at Vannes.

Paul Aurelian   Paul Aurelian or Pol de Léon was a 6th century bishop, one of the few British Celtic saints of whom a life exists written before AD 1000. It was completed in 884 by a Breton monk Wrmonec in the monastery of Landévennec in Brittany. Paul Aurelian was the son of a chieftain in South Wales and educated at the monastery of St Illtud at Llanwit Major where his comrades included Dewi Sant, Samson and Gildas. He took twelve followers and migrated to Brittany via Cornwall where he visited his sister Sitofolla (q.v.) at Mount's Bay. According to Wrmonec, he felt his sister and her companions were in an unsuitable place and acquired for them a new location on the edge of Gwavas Lake, Newlyn. Near Newlyn, of course, is the place he left his own name — Paul. The ancient church of Paul is dedicated to him, although there was a later confusion with St Paulinus of York, whose feastday is 10 October, whereas St Paul's is 12 March. Going on to Brittany, Paul established himself on the island of Batz, having supposedly expelled a dragon from the island, and was later consecrated the bishop of Léon. The town of St Pol de Léon was made the first bishopric in Lower Brittany. A small Celtic handbell from the 6th century, which survives here, is said to be that used by Paul himself. It is kept at the saint's shrine. Paul is reported to have died at an advanced age on the island of Batz.

Petroc   A 6th century abbot, Petroc was one of the outstanding British Celtic saints. His name survives in place-names and dedications in Wales, Somerset, Devon and Brittany as well as Cornwall. He originated in South Wales (in Dyfed there are St Petrox and Llanbedrog) and migrated to the Camel estuary of Cornwall where Padstow (Petroc's stow) became the chief centre of his missionary activities. Through several medieval Lives, a good deal of information is thought to be known about Petroc. He was uncle to Cadoc. He is said to have made a pilgrimage to Rome and to Jerusalem and lived a while on an island in the Indian Ocean. In his last years he retired to a hermitage on Bodmin Moor called Bosvenagh (the dwelling of monks). When he died, he was buried at Padstow. By the 11th century, Bodmin had become a centre of veneration for Petroc and his relics were housed there. Then in 1177 a disgruntled canon stole them and presented them to the abbey of Saint-Méen in Brittany. Henry II had to intervene to retrieve them for Bodmin. Petroc's feastday is 4 June.

Piala   A sister of Gwinear (q.v.) Piala was one of the Irish missionaries who landed at the Hayle estuary and was killed by Tewdrig. However, she gave her name to Phillack, near Hayle, and was remembered until the dedication was changed to St Felicity, a Roman martyr during the time of Antoninus Pius. The church at Phillack has an ancient chi-rho symbol now built into the south porch of the rebuilt (19th century) church.

Pinnock   Nothing is known of this saint, recorded as 'Sancti Pynnoch' in 1291. He/she gave the name to the parish of St Pinnock.

Piran   Sometimes given as Perran or Pirran. He was a 6th century abbot who came to be regarded as the patron saint of tinners and the national saint of Cornwall. The Cornish flag carries St Piran's Cross, a white cross on a black background. His feastday on 5 March has become a special Cornish day. Unfortunately the medieval *Life of St Piran* is simply an adaptation of the *Life of St Ciaran of Saighir*. There was a medieval chapel of St Piran in Cardiff but whether he came from south Wales is impossible to tell. He was also widely celebrated in Brittany where Saint-Perran stands south of Saint-Brieuc. He is also venerated by a shrine and statue in Trézélidé. In Cornwall, he is commemorated is several places such as Perranporth, where he is supposed to have founded his first church, Perranzabuloe, Perranarworthal and Perranuthnoe. During the Middle Ages there was a shrine at Perranzabuloe where the saint's relics were kept and which was one of the three important places of pilgrimage of Cornwall. As late as the reign of Elizabeth I, the skull of Piran together with his staff and a copper bell were preserved but they disappeared by the beginning of the 17th century. In spite of his being the most popular saint in Cornwall, because of the mixing of his traditions with St Ciaran, nothing is really known of his life and work.

Pratt   The church at Blisland, west of Bodmin Moor, has long locally been called St Pratt's, who it was argued was a forgotten Celtic saint. It seems that St Adwen (q.v.) was venerated here before St Pratt and some have argued that Pratt may be the Roman martyr named Protus who, with Hyacinth, was put to death by fire. A feastday for Pratt is celebrated on 11 September, which is the feastday of Protus and Hyacinth, to whom the church is now officially dedicated.

Probus   It is thought that Probus was an early Celtic Christian in the age before the spread of the Celtic Church and its saints. Probus, five miles east of Truro, to which he gave his name, has a church dedicated to St Probus and his wife St Grace. Two skulls were found in a recess wall of the sanctuary during restoration in 1851 and these are presumed to be the skulls of the saints. They are still kept in the church. Records show that there was an ancient monastery here which was reorganised after the English conquest.

Ruan   Ruan's dedications are to be found at Ruan Lanihorne, on the Fal, and at Ruan Major and Ruan Minor on the Lizard. He is also honoured in Devon where, at the great abbey of Tavistock, a shrine containing his relics stood. He is believed to have been a monk at Glastonbury and a companion of Kea (q.v.). His feastday is 30 August; a medieval *Life of St Ruan* is unfortunately an adaptation of the Breton St Ronan, an altogether different person.

Samson   Perhaps one of the most famous abbot-bishops of the Celtic church period, born c. 490 in South Wales, died c. 565 in Dol, Brittany. He is venerated at Golant just north of Fowey (where the church is particularly beautiful), and at Southill, the mother church of Callington. It is thought that the *Life of St Samson of Dol* is the earliest surviving biography of a British Celtic saint, being written within half-a-century of his death. His father was a chieftain named Amon of Dyfed and his mother was Anna of Gwent. He was educated and ordained at St Illtud's school at Llanilltud Fawr (Llanwit Major). He was abbot at Caldey Island and later visited Ireland. At a place on the banks of the Severn, in Dumnonia, he was consecrated a bishop by St Dubricius. He then moved into central Cornwall and visited Lan Docco (see the entry for St Kew). He went on to Brittany and acquired a reputation as a political negotiator between Judual, the ruler of Brittany, and the Frankish king Childebert I. He became bishop of Dol and thereby a significant founding father of the Breton Church. He attended the Council of Paris in AD 557. His feastday is 28 July.

Sancreed   The parish of Sancreed in West Penwith, does not take its name from St Creed. Sancreed is a complete name — St Sancreed. According to a medieval source he accidentally killed his father and, in a fit of remorse, went to work as a hermit/swineherd. In this way he was able to commune with God and start a ministry.

Sativola   See Sitofolla.

Selevan   Selevan appears as the son of St Erbyn, the grandson of St Geraint (Gerent) and the father of St Cuby. It has been suggested that Selevan, his brother Just and sister Silwen were all members of a prominent Cornish family who espoused Christianity in the same way as the children of Brychan. The church at St Levan, a half mile west of Porthcurno, is dedicated to St Selevan, and nearby still is a holy well and the ruins of what is claimed as the saint's original chapel. The place itself gets its name not from a separate saint called Levan but from a slurring of St Selevan into St Levan. There is some confusion as it is sometimes mistakenly thought that a St Levan gave his name to Porthleven (see Elwyn). Legends of Selevan were popular until recent times. Local fishermen used to call young sea bream or chad 'chuck-cheeld' (choke-child): it was said that when Selevan was visited by his sister with her two children, he served them up two chad as a meal. At first they turned up their noses at the fish but hunger overcame their fastidiousness and they ate them. But such was their haste that they choked on the bones. One bench end in the church has two fish carved on it.

Senan   St Senan gave his name to Sennan Cove. The church, the most westerly on the island of Britain, is dedicated to St Senana. It would seem that this was the 6th century Irish saint who was abbot of the monastery of Scattery (Inis Cathaig) on the Shannon. The monastery was famous for its learning throughout the Celtic world. He visited Dewi Sant in Wales and his feastday is celebrated on 8 March.

Senara   Zennor, four miles west of St Ives, is famous for its mermaid legend, for its memorial to 'John Davey (1812 – 1891) of Boswednack in this parish . . . who was the last to possess any considerable traditional knowledge of the Cornish language' and for the brief stay there of D.H. Lawrence and his wife, formerly Frieda von Richthofen: they were thought by the suspicious locals to be signalling to German U-Boats and driven out of the district. Yet of the female saint that gave the place her name, nothing is known. An ancient holy well survives at Venton Zennor under Zennor Carn.

Sithney   This seems to be the Breton Saint Sezni of whom a medieval Life survives — although it confuses the saint with Ciaran of Ireland. When William of Worcester visited Cornwall in the 15th century he reported that the burial place of St Sithney was still venerated at the church which bears his name near Helston. His feastday is 4 August.

Sitofolla   The sister of St Paul Aurelian (q.v.) who was resident at Mount's Bay when he visited her. She undoubtedly was the same person as St Sativola of Laneast, Launceston, and gave her name to Sidwell, a suburb of Exeter. Her feastday is 2 August.

Stediana   Remembered only as the female saint who is venerated at Stithians; also recorded as Stethyana.

Sulian   Dedications to Sulian, Suliau and Sulinus are to be found in Wales and Brittany as well as the name barely surviving in recognisable form in the place-name of Luxulyan (pronounced Lukzil'lian) where the church is now dedicated to SS Cyricus and Julitta and a little more recognisably at Tresillian near Truro.

Teath   St Teath, whose name is sometimes rendered as Tetha or Tedda, is listed as one of Brychan's children. She gave her name to the village which is three miles south-west of Camelford. In the church dedicated to her is an intriguing 16th century pulpit bearing the Carminow arms and the motto in Cornish *Cala : Rag : Whetlow* (a straw for the tale-bearer). There is also an old Celtic high cross in the churchyard. The parish was the birthplace of the notorious Captain William Bligh of the Bounty. Teath shares a feastday with one of the four great pagan Celtic festivals — 1 May.

Tudy   St Tudy is the village where William Bligh (see above) spent his childhood. The church is dedicated to St Uda, a form of Tudy. He is thought to have been a friend of Brioc and went to Brittany with him for his name appears on the Breton coast, not far from Saint-Brieuc, at le Tudy and Loctudy. His feastday is on 11 May.

Tugdual   Although no longer venerated in Cornwall, Tugdual deserves a mention in a list of Cornish saints as a 6th century Cornishman who is still venerated in Brittany. The cathedral of St Tugdual at Tréguier is one of the finest Breton cathedrals; the current building dates to the 13th-15th centuries. Whilst Cornish and Breton tradition claims him as Cornish, he is also claimed for Wales and his name is perpetuated on the Lleyn peninsula.

Uda   See Tudy.

Uny   See Euny.

Veep   It is uncertain whether St Veep was male or female. The name survives in St Veep above Penpoll Creek on the lower Fowey. In the 14th century the church there was re-dedicated to SS Cyricus and Julitta.

Veryan   See Buryan.

Wendron   Remembered as 'Sancte Wendrone' in 1291. The parish of Wendron takes its name from him, although there is an argument that Wendron might have been female as the name is given feminine form as 'St Wendrona' in another source.

Wenna   Wenna was another of Brychan's daughters. St Wenn in north Cornwall takes its name from her and the church at Morval, near East Looe, is dedicated to her. Her feast day is 18 October.

Wennap   See Gwennap.

Wethinoc   Wethinoc was a hermit visited by Petroc at Padstow. He gave up his hermitage to Petroc who founded a monastery at the site, which became Petroc's stow (Padstow).

Willow   Willow, sometimes spelt Wyllow or Wylloc, was an Irish missionary who established his hermitage at Pont Pill. In the 15th century William of Worcester tells us that Lanteglos-by-Fowey was dedicated to him. A chapel dedicated to St Willow also stood at Lamelin, the site of which is a farm; it was at this spot, it was said, that he met martyrdom. The story goes that Willow was slain by an evil person named Melyn, who in some versions of the tale is described as his brother. The medieval tale says that after he was beheaded, Willow picked up his head and carried it to the site where St Willow was built.

Winnoc   A Welshman, sometimes given as Winnow, he went to Cornwall and established a church on the Fowey just below Lostwithiel, where the church is dedicated to him. He died in 715 so his dates are rather later than the majority of Celtic saints in Cornwall. He went to the continent, probably via Brittany, and joined Bertin of Coutances (died c.700). Bertin selected Winnoc, with three Celtic companions, to establish a monastery at Wormhoudt, near Dunkirk. Winnoc's name appears in many medieval calendars. His feastday was 6 November.

Winnow   See Winnoc.

Winwaloe   See Gunwalloe.

Wolvela   See Gulval.

Wron   See Goran.

Zennor   See Senara.

Selected Gazetteer

Place or dedication	See under Saint:	Saint's day
Advent	Adwen	
Altarnun	Non	15 June
Blisland	Pratt	11 September
Bodmin	Goran	7 April
Breage	Breaca	4 June
Budock	Budoc	8 December
Camborne	Meryadoc	
Cardingham	Meubred	
Colan	Colan	20 May
Constantine	Constantine	9 March
Crantock	Crantock	
Crowan	Crowan	
Cubert	Cubert	
Cury	Corentin	12 December
Davidstow	Dewi	1 March
Egloskerry	Keria	
Feock	Feock	2 February
Fowey	Fimbarrus	25 September
Germoe	Germoe	24 June
Gerrans	Gerent	
Golant	Samson	28 July
Gulval	Gulval	
Gunwalloe	Gunwalloe	3 March
Gwennap	Gwennap	1 July
Gwinear	Gwinear	23 March
Gwithian	Gwithian	
Harlyn Bay	Buryan	4 June
Illogan	Illogan	
Kea	Kea	3 October
Ladock	Ladoca	
Landewednack	Gunwalloe	3 March
Laneast	Sativola	2 August
Lanhydrock	Hydroc	5 May
Lanivet	Nevet	
Lanivet	Congar	
Lanlivery	Bryvyth	
Lanreath	Manacca	14 October

Lansallas	Ildierna	
Lanteglos	Juliot	16 June
Lanteglos	Willow	
Lamorran	Morenna	
Lelant	Anta	
Lelant	Euny	1 February
Lostwithiel	Winnoc	6 November
Linkinhorne	Mylor	1 October
Ludgvan	Ludgvan	
Luxulyan	Sulian	29 July
Madron	Madron	17 May
Mawes	Mawes	18 November
Mawgan-in-Pydar	Mawgan	24 September
Mawgan-in-Meneage	Mawgan	24 September
Mawnan	Mawnan	24 September
Menheniot	Neot	31 July
Merther	Coan	
Mevagissey	Issey	
Mevagissey	Mevan	
Minver	Minver	
Morwenstow	Morwenna	8 July
Morval	Wenna	18 October
Mullion	Mullion	
Mylor	Mylor	1 October
Newlyn East	Neulina	
Padstow	Petroc	4 June
Paul	Paul Aurelian	12 June
Perranporth	Piran	5 March
Perranarworthal	Piran	5 March
Perranuthnoe	Piran	5 March
Perranzabuloe	Piran	5 March
Petherwin	Pattern	
Phillack	Piala	14 December
Philleigh	Fili	
Pont Pill (Fowey)	Willow	
Porthleven	Elwyn	22 February
Probus	Probus	5 July
Redruth	Euny	1 February
Roche	Gonand	
Ruan Lanihorne	Ruan	30 August
Ruan Major	Ruan	30 August
Ruan Minor	Ruan	30 August

St Allen	Allen	13 January
St Austell	Austell	28 June
St Breock	Brioc	1 May
St Breward	Breward	19 January
St Buryan	Buryan	4 June
St Cleer	Cleer	4 November
St Clether	Clether	4 November
St Columb Major	Columb	13 November
St Columb Minor	Columb	13 November
St Creed (Grampound)	Crida	
St Day	Day	18 January
St Endellion	Endelienta	29 April
St Enoder	Enoder	27 April
St Enodoc (Padstow)	Enodoc	7 March
St Erth	Erth	31 October
St Erme	Erbyn	13 January
St Erney	Erney	
St Ervan	Erbyn	13 January
St Eval	Eval	20 November
St Ewe	Ewe	
St Gennys	Gennys	2 May
St Germans	Germanus	31 July
St Gluvias (by Penryn)	Gluvias	3 May
St Goran	Goran	6 April
St Ingonger	Congar	
St Issey	Issey	
St Ive	Ivo	24 April
St Ives	Ia	3 February
St Juliot (Boscastle)	Juliot	16 June
St Kenwyn	Kenwyn	
St Keverne	Keverne	18 November
St Kew	Docco	
St Kew	Kew	8 January
St Keyne	Keyne	8 October
St Levan	Selevan	25 June
St Mabyn	Mabyn	18 November
St Mawes	Mawes	18 November
St Mellion	Mellion	6 November
St Mellion	Mullion	6 January
St Merryn	Merryn	7 July
St Mewan	Mewan	21 June
St Minver	Minver	24 November

St Nectan's Chapel	Nectan	17 June
St Nectan's Glen	Nectan	17 June
St Neot	Neot	31 July
St Neot	Gueryr	4 April
St Nighton	Nectan	17 June
St Pinnock	Pinnock	6 November
St Sithney	Sithney	4 August
St Teath	Teath	1 May
St Tudy	Tudy	11 May
St Veep	Veep	1 July
St Wenn	Wenna	18 October
St Winnow	Winnoc	6 November
Sancreed	Sancreed	
Sennan Cove	Senan	8 March
Stithians	Stediana	
Southill	Samson	28 July
Terney	Erney	
Towednack	Gunwalloe	3 March
Tremaine	Gunwalloe	3 March
Trevena	Merteriana	9 April
Veryan	Buryan	4 June
Washaway	Conan	23 July
Wendron	Wendron	
Zennor	Senara	